Thank you to the following individuals, without their contributions and support this book would not have been written:

Sahana Holla – my wife, for reviewing the book and suggesting changes, and taking care of the family.

Roshan and Rishita – my children, for being patient while I was working on the book.

U.K.Maiya and Geetha – my parents, for giving me the highest level of education, guidance, experience.

My mentors in corporate world and professional world – A. Rafeq, Anil Kumar, R. Rajan, Nauzer Gotla, Noel Heredia.

OS Hardware

Product Development Process for Open Source Hardware

Girish Maiya

This book is published as a reference guide for OSH professionals and enthusiasts. Any reference to specific products or company is only to help out in product development process. The intention is not to promote or disregard any product or company.

For information contact; ugirishm@yahoo.com
Book and Cover design by Girish Maiya

Publisher: titbox.in

ISBN: 978-93-5212-646-0

First Edition: April 2015

Contents

CHAPTER 1

Introduction

In recent times, open source hardware products are becoming very common in the marketplace, and many new products are in different stages of development, which are expected to hit the market soon. There are many reasons for such phenomenal growth in open source hardware and in future it is expected to increase even further. Some of the important factors that are helping this exponential growth of product development using open source hardware approach are mentioned below:

1. Introduction of cheap, easy to configure, easy to program microprocessors under the brand Arduino. Huge number of Arduino compatible components are also being introduced, which is contributing towards increase in projects and products using Arduino microprocessors. This is not only leading to many DIY type of projects but also many popular products for commercial purpose.

2. Development of self-replicating 3D printers named RepRap, as well as free availability of complex designs that can be used by these printers. This is

helping in providing many mechanical features controlled by open source hardware components. Even though only plastic printer heads are available currently, the printer has already become a major contributor towards development of new open source products. Once printer heads for different materials are made available, it could propel this new phenomenon even further.

3. Renewed enthusiasm in the crowd-funding space has given rise to many new ideas being funded by the public, who are now open to take the risk. Open source hardware is used by these idea generators for developing their products as the product development cost is lesser and the ability to perform accelerated product development. Ease of creating new campaigns, ease of marketing them, ease of getting funded through simple online tools provided by the new crowd-funding companies are driving this new enthusiasm.

Since there are no well-documented processes for open source hardware product development, these developers are trying to adapt the traditional product development process. However, as they gain more experience, they try to follow some form of informal process based on their experience, since the traditional process cannot be followed for open source hardware product development. These informal processes followed by different developers needs to be consolidated, structured and documented, so that the product developers can follow a well-structured process as well as introduce process improvements as the open source hardware industry matures in the future.

In this article, an attempt has been done to document the product development process followed for open source hardware (OSH) based on extensive research and online discussions and experiences mentioned in various forums to capture the different informal processes being followed. Differences between OSH product development and traditional product development process, along with the advantages and disadvantages of the OSH product development process, are also captured in this article. A case study is also included which can be referenced for practical implementation of the process or to refer to a practical example when the concepts are not very clear. Interesting topics like OSH companies, enablers, products, funding, licensing, trends etc. are included for readers' benefit.

This book is intended for reference by OSH product developers to follow a standardized and consistent process. Companies developing OSH product can also use this book for implementing formal process within their company. OSH enthusiasts can also use this article to understand more about the OSH product development process and other useful information. Interesting concepts and case studies are included to increase the awareness of OSH based product development and to encourage readers to get into open source hardware, if they are not actively involved currently.

Since this a new area with lots of development happening very rapidly, there could be changes happening to the information included in this article. The research will be continued and as and when there are significant changes, new version of this article will be published. Also, additional topics will be included in the article in future that could be of interest to the OSH community.

One of objectives of some of the OSH component developers is 'to make electronics easy and fun'. Similarly, the objective of this book is 'to make reading about hardware easy and fun'. Hence the format and language of this book is kept informal, simple and easy cross referable between chapters.

CHAPTER 2

What and Why OSH

Most of us would be aware of the concept of open source mainly due to the popularity of open source software during the last decade. 'Open Source' means everything that is available for sharing pertaining to a product is shared and made available to everyone for their use and there is no legal binding on its usage. In software world design, documents, source code are all digital and hence it can be made open in entirety. However, in open source hardware, only the documentation is digital but the actual product is physical. Hence for open source hardware design and other documents relating to the product are open. Apart from this OSH professionals also share lots of knowledge about the products, which is giving it true open characteristics. Actual manufacturing or assembling of the product still needs to be done by the individuals and there is cost associated with this activity, which is the main difference between open source software and open source hardware.

To summarize, open source hardware is a product where in the design, source code for programs and other documents are made public and anyone is allowed to use it for producing or assembling their own product. Table #1 shows the differences between open source software and open source hardware. It is clear from this table that most of the requirement for open source software and hardware are similar where the items involved are mostly digital in nature. For physical product related to hardware, since each copy will have a cost for reproducing it, there is a cost associated with it and hence that is collected from the user along with a small amount of profit.

Items	Open Source	
	Software	Hardware
Idea Details	Open/Free	Open/Free
Requirement Details	Open/Free	Open/Free
Design Documents	Open/Free	Open/Free
Prototypes	Open/Free	Price payable
Instructions	Open/Free	Open/Free
Product	Open/Free	Price payable

Open/Free   Price payable

Table #1: comparison of open source software with open source hardware.

Table #2 shows the difference between traditional product development and OSH. Here since both are hardware, the items involved are same. However, in traditional method, digital items are subjected to copyrights and physical product is protected through patenting and intellectual property rights. In open source these materials are all open but only the cost is payable for the physical product.

Items	Traditional	OSH
Idea Details	©	
Requirement Details	©	
Design Documents	©	
Prototypes	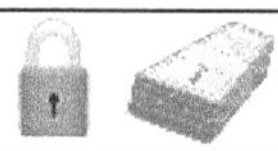	
Instructions	©	
Product	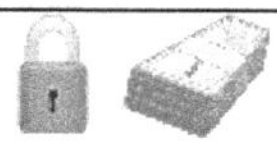	

 Open/Free

 Price payable

© Copyright

 Patented

Table #2: comparison of traditional process with open source hardware.

Now that we have understood what open source hardware is, let's try to understand why it is important. The shared documentation and the knowledge, which is the key attribute of OSH, allows for collaborative and incremental product development and innovation, which in turn is leading to accelerated product development. This attribute is very important for a world that drives on a fast lane, and would like to see new products and upgrades within a smaller time-frame. Apart from the above mentioned, lets also look at some of the attributes of OSH which will help us to understand why we need OSH.

The important aspects of OSH that makes it growing

phenomenon are given below:

1. **Knowledge based:**

OSH is based on collaborative, incremental innovation through shared knowledge. Those countries that have huge pool of knowledge resources and an appetite for new idea generation and implementation can easily contribute to OSH based product development and production. The trend is towards making easily configurable hardware that can be controlled through software programs. Countries having good number software resources can also easily progress into product development that requires hardware-software combination.

2. **Inexpensive products:**

In OSH world, since the products are developed through collaboration and incremental innovation, there is negligible or no cost related to research, design and development, which in-turn will reduce the product cost and price significantly. The goal of OSH based approach is to bring the price down to about 10% of the current price, which will mostly be the manufacturing cost. Overheads and other indirect costs like sales and marketing etc. will be very minimal. The product pricing will be mostly based on cost plus approach, which will mostly include only manufacturing cost. All the above mentioned factors will lead to a variety of new products introduced into the market that are very cheap to produce and purchase.

3. **Reduction in distribution and inventory cost:**

OSH also promotes local, on-demand and flexible manufacturing. This is different from the current practice of importing from outside location or manufacturing at a central location and then spending large amount in transportation and warehousing. OSH also promotes recycling junks and other raw materials which ensure better usage of locally available resources. This also encourages countries to better manage their local resources as they'll have local demand for them. For countries that imports huge amount of fuel, this would be highly beneficial as lower distribution cost would lead to lower requirement for fuel used in transportation.

4. **Educative and fun:**

Recent trend in OSH world is to make electronics easy to learn, implement and innovate. There are also efforts to make it a fun experience. As electronics starts to become a fun and easy experience, it will be easy to incorporate OSH based training and projects in institutions and organizations. This in turn will increase the availability of highly skilled resources in hardware and manufacturing domain. OSH enthusiast will be able to take up DIY type of projects on their own easily and students can do many interesting projects for their school work.

5. **Accelerated product development:**

Collaboration and knowledge sharing is also enabling accelerated product development. Instead of individuals or teams spending huge effort in taking an idea all the way till producing a marketable products, networked teams across the world are able to contribute in their own way to OSH based product development. Incremental development approach, reuse of huge repository of knowledge materials and experiences is also contributing to accelerated product development. For products that used to take years earlier to get them to marketplace are now hitting the market within few months.

6. **Become a better engineer:**

The new mindset with product developers and engineers is that, instead of getting richer by maintaining secrecy of the ideas and products, its' good to become a better engineer by disclosing the details to public and getting feedback. Once you open up the idea, design or other materials, you'll get positive as well as negative feedback, which can be used to fine tune your product as well as your skills. If you are working for a big company using traditional way of product development, you don't get exposure to all the phases of product development. In OSH approach you have a chance to work in all the areas, which also helps in becoming a better engineer.

From the above points it's clear as to what aspects of OSH are making it a new phenomenon and also why it is required. It is better to get on to this new phenomenon early, and hence it is suggested that the readers use this book as a guide for first step into OSH.

CHAPTER 3

Product development process for OSH

Since open source hardware is relatively a new concept, most of the OSH product developers have been applying traditional product development approach, but due to the very nature of OSH, a different process needs to be followed. In practice, OSH enthusiasts and professionals have been following different steps based on their experience and those that meet the requirements of OSH product development. However, they are not very structured and not followed consistently. There is a requirement for consolidating these practices, provide a structure and share a well-documented process with OSH community for being reused. Based on extensive research on the nature of OSH, experiences mentioned by enthusiasts and professionals in online forums, a structured process has been developed and documented in this book, that can be followed for OSH product development. As OSH is a recent phenomenon, the process could change in future as the concepts gets fine-tuned, settles down and becomes more matured in future. The changes happening in the OSH world will be monitored regularly and with the help of SMEs in OSH further fine-tuning and updates to the process will be done on a regular basis. Below is the diagrammatic representation of the OSH process and various components or phases within the process.

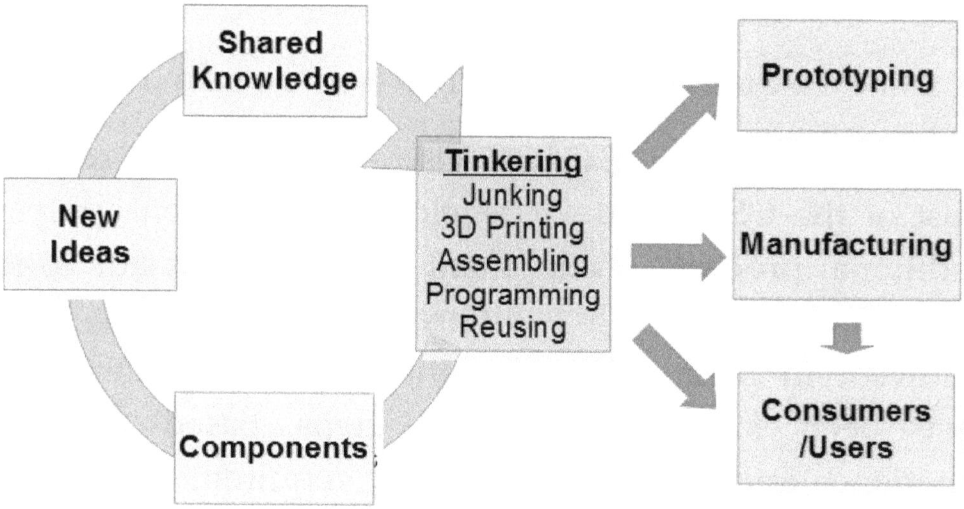

1. **Shared knowledge**

In this phase, the designs and other documents that are developed during product development are shared with everyone. Technical know-how, specifications and any other important information and instructions are also published for sharing the knowledge with the whole open source community. These artifacts can be used by anyone for their own use or for commercial purpose based on the type of open source license applied on them. Currently there is no central body which is enabling, promoting or providing a central repository for knowledge sharing and hence scattered all over the place, especially on the internet.

This is an additional step in OSH product development aided through online knowledge sharing. For each and every step in the product development, the knowledge you gain is shared with others. This is the core of open source approach where in all the details of your product is made public so that it can used by others. In the same manner you can browse through designs and other materials shared by others and see if it can be used in your product. This is in contrary to traditional product development where in the knowledge and other details are kept secret to enable patenting, IP rights and copyrights.

2. **New idea generation**

In this phase new ideas are generated and shared with the OSH community. This is probably taken up as the first step, however as knowledge sharing happens during all the phases, we have mentioned that step in the beginning. It can be a completely new idea requiring initiation of a new project or could be small incremental idea on any existing product or project. Ideas could be coming from a wide range of sources, starting from a domain expert to a common man who may or may not be related to the product or project. The idea could also be a generic functionality that could be included in any product.

This step in OSH approach is same as in traditional

product development however the mindset and volume of ideas would be different. In traditional product development only people who are responsible for new ideas or those who are a bit entrepreneurial would be generating new ideas and taking it to the next level. In OSH approach everyone will have a mindset of looking out for new ideas and will be doing it constantly and applying it on everything. The main reason for this is collaborative and incremental idea generation and product development attribute that comes with OSH approach. People can share incremental ideas to an existing project or as a complete new project mainly on online forums, social networking groups, blogs etc. OSH volunteers will be browsing through the shared ideas to screen them for further processing and follow-up with idea generator for any additional details required. Once the idea is shared and validated, OSH enthusiasts will start contributing towards the new idea. The enthusiasts will be able to provide feedback about the ideas or can add onto the idea. They'll be able to direct the community to anything already being done similar to the idea and also suggest any other areas where the same idea can be applied. High level designs or abstracts are also made available so that it is easier to collaborate. Due to the active participation of users and other stakeholders, it would be pretty much clear at this stage itself whether the product will be popular or not, where as in traditional approach you'll get to know about it only at latter stages.

3. **Components**

OSH based innovation and manufacturing includes assembling of lots of cheap components. These components are themselves manufactured based on OSH approach and then they'll be used in other products. The components could vary from a small microprocessor, to different kinds of sensors, to even very small components like capacitors.

These components are not only becoming cheaper but very easy to use as well. Based on the requirement of your product you'll have to identify appropriate components. There are OSH components kits available in the market which usually has most of the commonly used components. It is suggested to regularly browse through the components available, as many times you could get new ideas by looking at the features available in these components. In this phase you'll only identify the components that are required by your product. As you move ahead with next few steps you'll get to know as to which ones you'll have to buy and which ones are available for use. In case you plan to buy them, there are many online stores that sell cheap OSH components which can be explored, including component kits.

4. Tinkering

This is the phase where actual innovation, product design and development happens. Once enough feedback is received for the new idea and if sufficient interest is shown, OSH enthusiasts will start taking it up for further processing. Entrepreneurs and corporates also might take up some really interesting ideas for further development. Depending on their bandwidth the OSH enthusiasts will contribute towards the design and product development. Depending on their expertise, knowledge, interest areas they might take up specific task within the design and development process. Some of the activities within this phase are described here.

Junking is an activity where products that are thrown away are hacked into to understand the working of those products. Also, parts that are working well are removed for reuse in other product development. This step can be followed on a regular basis to build your repository of components fished out of junks.

3D printing is an activity where in shared designs are fed into a OSH based 3D printer to produce either the whole product or parts to be used in the product. Designs are altered as per the requirement to print various alternatives of the products or parts. Different designs are tried out to identify the best among them.

Assembling is a task where in junked parts, 3D printed parts and other components or parts are put together to form the complete product. Depending on the product requirements, the parts and components are assembled using different assembling tools and processes.

Final part is the **programming** of the assembled product. The current trend is to make the task till assembling easy, and then giving higher programming ability, so that product design and requirements can be altered easily through software itself, instead of making painstaking changes in the hardware. This brings in flexibility to the hands of developers, who can play around with different features and functionality with very few changes in hardware and making most of the changes in software.

5. Prototyping

Once the product is developed and initial checks are done it needs to be thoroughly tested to ensure there are no defects. Once the design is ready and some kind of initial working model is tested out, detailed prototypes need to be manufactured for extensive testing as well as user feedback. In OSH approach, prototypes are manufactured through the tinkering process itself, where in cheap components are used and also old components are reused for prototyping.

Also, the contributors, users and testers across the world build their own prototypes using the information shared by the product developers and hence the cost is shared between many people. Prototyping is one of the ways for continuous, incremental development combined with testing and feedback from the user communities.

Collaboration and shared knowledge makes this process easy and effective. The prototypes need to be tested extensively and feedback needs to be obtained from the user community. This is an important phase in product development to ensure the product works as per expectation without any defect and also to validate if the product functionality meets the user expectations.

6. **Manufacturing**

Once the product is tested, features and functionalities finalized and packaged, it needs to be manufactured for the use of consumers. The design and other specifications, documents etc. will be made available for anyone to manufacture the product on their own for self-use or for commercial purpose. Due to on-demand and localized production requirement for OSH products, traditional manufacturing options may not be appropriate. The OSH based products, upon receipt of an order by the customer, will be produced at local manufacturing units that allow for flexible and scale-able manufacturing. The manufacturing units, assemblers and packagers need to be available at different locations to take care of local markets. Depending on the ordered quantity either small, medium or large scale manufacturing option can be selected.

7. **Consumers and users**

Like any other product development, the last phase is the consumption of the product by consumers or users. Like the usual path, the products could be sold once it is manufactured, if a manufacturing vendor is selected for the product. In OSH based approach, the product could also move directly from tinkering phase to the consumers without moving into manufacturing phase, as OSH enthusiasts or professionals can sell the products by tinkering them in small batches to meet small local requirements.

OSH enthusiasts will work with leading online product sellers to provide an option to get orders for products through their websites. Once the order is received through these websites, it would be routed to a manufacturer in the same location as the user, who produces it and delivers it to the user.

Apart from developing various OSH based products for the user community, OSH based tools and equipment to be used in the manufacturing process will also be developed. This will reduce the investment to be made in manufacturing facilities and will reduce the manufacturing cost further. These tools and equipment can be used for manufacturing non-OSH products as well, which will benefit traditional manufacturing industry as well.

From the above structured process for OSH product development, you can see that it is completely different than traditional product development process. Following the above process will make the product development in OSH very effective, repeatable, consistent, standardized and fast.

CHAPTER 4

Difference from traditional process

It is beneficial to understand the differences between traditional product development and manufacturing and of OSH based product development and manufacturing process. It would be beneficial to understand the similarities as well to leverage the existing processes within your organization. Sometimes your situation might require you to adapt steps from traditional process along with other OSH processes. Your understanding of the concepts related to OSH process would also become better by going through the differences, advantages and disadvantages in comparison to traditional process. Based on the experience and industry there could be different variants of the traditional approach. This book has tried to generalize the process as much as possible so that it's easier to understand conceptually and also to compare it with OSH process. Generalizing also helps to come up with advantages, disadvantages, similarities and differences. The idea here is to understand the OSH approach better by comparing it to other process and not really to become a master in traditional approach.

Below is a high level diagrammatic representation of the

traditional product development and manufacturing process.

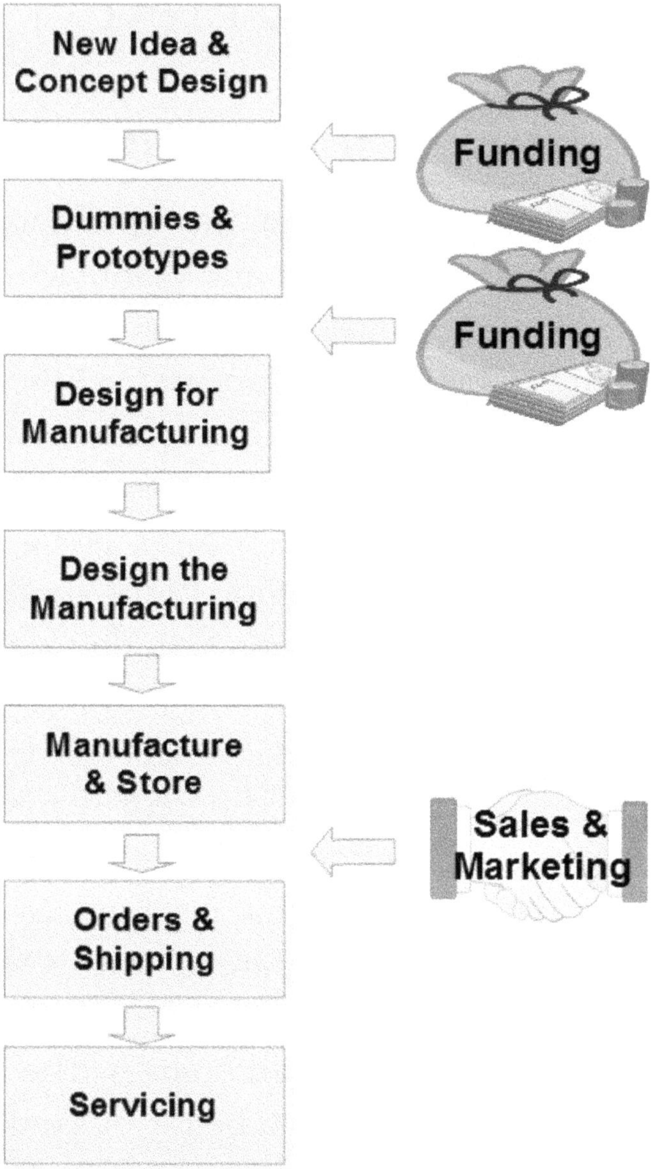

Apart from bringing out the details of the steps, its differences and advantages to OSH is also brought out in the below sections. Where ever required similarities and disadvantages is also made clear.

1. **New idea based on an issue or requirement:**

   When a person or corporate faces an issue or opportunity they come up with an idea to cater to that issue or opportunity. A new idea could come up through visualization of applying an existing or new technology for a different purpose. In traditional approach the new idea is not published much or shared within a closed group. There is no collaboration and only minimal validation of the idea at this stage. The objective is to generate ideas for products that can be developed and sold for making huge profit. Even though this step is same as OSH based process, the difference is in maintaining the details confidential in traditional process versus sharing everything in OSH approach.

2. **Concept design based on new idea:**

   After the idea has gone through discussions with closed groups and minimal validation, some kind of concept design is developed. This will give a visual representation of the new idea or the product. The main purpose of the design is to make use of it for the demonstration of the idea to the stakeholders and also for a high level validation of the idea. The design is done by the idea generators themselves or with the help of a small design team. In OSH approach this step is optional and usually done in the tinkering stage, while performing the assembly or other sub-steps. Some times its included in idea generation stage itself, so that appropriate feedback can be received from others. If you are developing a complex product, you might opt for creating a concept design in the OSH process as well.

3. **Funding for developing:**

Since a team will have to spend considerable time as well as investment is required for taking the product from concept stage to make it manufacture-able, funding is required for the same. Many times individuals put in their own savings or borrow funds from friends or families. Some of them might go for internal corporate funding or approach venture capitalists or other investors. The latest trend is to go for crowd-funding. Since there is no collaboration or a easily available platform and infrastructure, the funding requirement is usually huge and many good ideas fallout because of lack of funds. In OSH based product development usually there is no need for funding at this stage or the need is very minimum. As the effort and resources are usually shared by contributors, the burden is spread out and hence becomes affordable by the contributors. Even if you need some funding it's easy to get crowd funding as the idea and product is already validated by the users by this time.

4. **Dummies based on the design:**

Some product developers go for creating dummies

before developing the prototype. It is to further validate the concept and idea. Sometimes stakeholders suggest for a demo using dummies before they decide on funding. In earlier step the idea or product would have a virtual shape through concept design whereas in this step it will take a raw physical shape with minimum to none functionality. Since prototyping is costly in traditional product development, this step is opted before going in for prototyping. This step can be completely eliminated in approaches where prototyping is cheap and easy. Also in OSH process in the tinkering stage you are developing a fully functional raw product, which eliminates the requirement to create a dummy.

5. **Prototypes and validations based on the design:**

Once funded, required materials are procured and a prototype is built based on the design. Once the prototype is checked by the developers it is sent out for validation by a separate team. Based on the feedback from validation team modifications might be required to the prototype. There could be multiple iterations between validation team and developers. Building prototypes and modifications to them are very costly. Absence of collaboration and well laid out platform are some of the reasons for making it a costly step. Also advantages of incremental development and sharing of experience and knowledge are also missing. This step is key for OSH based process as well. The difference is that, it's a cheaper process in OSH approach as you'll be mostly using cheap components that provide option to program most of the functionality, which in turn will help the developers to play around with a single piece of prototype. Also, the prototypes are built by the users and OSH enthusiasts themselves from the design and other shared materials. The prototypes are tested by potential users in OSH approach, eliminating the requirement for a dedicated validation team.

6. **Designing for manufacturing:**

The initial design and production methods might have to be changed for usage by the manufacturer. There are different methods that are followed by manufacturers, depending on the materials, product requirements, assembling process, maintainability, cost of production etc. Each of these methods will impose certain requirements and constraints on the design of the product and hence changes are required to the initial design. This could mean compromising on some of the features of the product. Cheap mass production methods many times could lead to non-optimum products. In OSH based development as you'll be going for on-demand and localized manufacturing, you might use small scale manufacturing process including home based manufacturing or even use the tinkering process itself. Hence the redesign requirement will be very minimal under these options.

7. **Funding for manufacturing:**

Once the design for manufacturing is ready, actual manufacturing, distribution, inventory, sales and marketing needs to start. All this require huge investment. Based on the costing, forecasting, estimates etc. detailed financial plan is put together including funding sources. Based on a detailed business plan, various funding agencies will be approached for investing in manufacturing of the product. Again, lack of collaboration and shared responsibilities, lack of established common platform etc. puts the burden on developers as it requires huge investment in traditional product development and manufacturing. As mentioned in the previous section, due to usage of on-demand and local manufacturing option for OSH products, the investment will be very minimal. So, the funding requirement will be very less and usually the consumers of the product are ready to make the payment in advance, which can be used towards manufacturing cost.

8. **Designing the manufacturing process:**

Based on the complexity of the product, equally complex manufacturing process might be required. Number of components, global locations and vendors, packaging options etc. could lead to further complex process. IP based products will require splitting up the products to make sure vendors are not able to replicate the product on their own and also for the company to take up key processes in-house to guard the product secrecy. It's an iterative process requiring lots of effort, time and money, and will require involvement of SMEs in this area. Non availability of local components and manufacturers makes it a very difficult process. Lack of collaboration, knowledge sharing and non-utilization of latest manufacturing technologies and processes makes it a very inefficient and ineffective task. For OSH products this step is either not required or will be very simple and hence clubbed along with the manufacturing process. Small scale, on-demand and localized production are the key reasons for making it a simple task under OSH based approach. Also, since there is no IP related issue, no additional strategy needs to be implemented in the manufacturing process.

9. **Working on manufacturing and logistics:**

Once you have designed the manufacturing process, you'll have to start working with various parties for implementing the process. You'll identify and start working with manufacturers, component sellers, parts vendors and people who assemble them, based on your design of the manufacturing process. Based on your inventory, distribution and marketing plans you'll also need to work with packaging service providers, warehouses and global shippers and distributors. Based on your experience in the phase you might have to modify your design of the manufacturing processes. This step could become tedious if your manufacturing process is complex. Many times the cost of manufacturing, components, parts, assembling them would be much lesser than all the other steps in the manufacturing process. Again, non-availability of local manufacturers and vendors, contributes to this task being inefficient and ineffective. Non-availability of on-demand manufacturing increases inventory and distribution costs. Similar to the earlier step, this is a simple task for OSH product and is usually a part of manufacturing process. Small scale, on-demand and localized production are the main reasons for making this step simple.

10. **Setting up sales and marketing:**

A sales and marketing team is required to sell the product developed through traditional process. Many times success of a product greatly depends on sales and marketing strategies. The strategy deployed will depend on the product category, competition, market type, budget available, sales channel etc. Experts will have to be brought in, to develop and implement the strategies. Again lack of collaboration, knowledge sharing, incremental product development makes it an unwanted critical and costly task. For OSH products, the requirement of sales and marketing is very less. Usually, the product would have already made a buzz even before it is developed due to active participation of users and other stakeholders from the early stage of the process. Free or cheap social media is used to make the product popular to the general public.

11. **<u>Taking orders and shipping the product:</u>**

Once the product is manufactured, depending on the requirement and effectiveness of marketing, customers will be ready to place orders for the products. You need to ensure that there are appropriate mechanisms available for your customers to buy your product or place an order for the product. There are various approaches for this step and based on your targeted customers, you need to select the right approach. The approach could also depend on the sector and nature of your product. The approach could be as simple as selling through retailers and distributors or through online tools, to complex turnkey based on detailed proposals. Products could fail if proper approach is not selected. Collaboration, shared knowledge, common established platform would make this task effective and cheap. For OSH based products, usually the users would manufacture the product on their own. For those products which require manufacturing by specialists, orders are taken in advance and then, based on the shipping location, produced at a facility closer to that location. Some simple products could be sold through street side shops or vendors, for which manufacturing is done on a daily basis locally based on the quantity of products sold during the day.

12. **<u>Servicing the product:</u>**

Once the product is sold and clients have started using it, if any issues occur or maintenance is required, it will have to be serviced. The manufacturers will have to setup a chain of service centers for this purpose. Trained resources and all parts and components will have to be made available in these centers. Some products might require on-site servicing. In traditional approach due to IP and other reasons many times the products are assembled in such a way that it is hard to open up and service the product. Non-availability of cheap components, parts, knowledge of the product makes servicing and maintenance a costly affair. For OSH products usually, the users themselves would be able to troubleshoot and fix the problems, as all the product details and instructions are released to the public, which can be used by them. Small service centers catering to all OSH products in general, would be able to do the troubleshooting and fixing on behalf of the users. As these products are very cheap they would usually become use and throw type of products and OSH junkyards would be put to good use for such products. Some of the products could have modular design so that you can replace specific modules in case of any issue, instead of replacing the whole product.

From these discussions it is clear that traditional product development is completely different from product development process for OSH. You can refer back to this chapter while going through the OSH process to understand the difference clearly or to check if any of the traditional steps would apply to your situation, when you are having issues implementing the OSH process.

CHAPTER 5

Advantages and Disadvantages of OSH process

In this chapter let us try to understand the advantages and disadvantages of product development using open source hardware approach. It is important to understand this to check if all the steps in OSH process are appropriate for your situation or you have to go for adapting some of the steps in traditional way of product development. The differences and advantages of OSH process in comparison with traditional process is already discussed in earlier chapter. Let us consolidate them here and also explain any other advantages. It is important to know the disadvantages as well, so that you are conscious about it while executing various steps and can have appropriate work around and mitigation plans.

Advantages of OSH based approach are listed below:

1. **Cheap product development process:**

   Due to the use of collaborative and incremental development approach the product development becomes a cheaper process than the traditional process. This will not only encourage many people to get into product development as they can afford it, but also ensure that the product that are developed using open source approach are cheaper. As mentioned in the earlier chapter many of the costly process steps that are followed in traditional approach are not applicable to OSH approach. Using cheap components, tools and equipment that are produced using OSH approach will further reduce the manufacturing cost. Other costs related to patenting and legal matters need not be incurred for OSH products. Funding requirement is also very minimal and usually can be absorbed by the contributors themselves, and users are ready to pay the product price in advance, which can be used for funding of product development as well as manufacturing them.

2. **Accelerated product development:**

Due to shared knowledge, experience and development tasks, OSH provides scope for accelerated product development. Applying incremental development approach also helps in release of product versions within expedited time-line. Due to the active feedback and contribution mechanism the product is validated early in the process and hence you get a sense as to how useful and popular the product will be. If a product is considered good many people will jump in and contribute to the product development. In case of any issues or road blocks you have a huge knowledge base and ready support available to resolve them. Also, instead of releasing product with full functionality at once, you could have multiple releases with incremental functionality. The iterations within the product development process is also quicker and faster due to contribution from many people with skill-sets in required areas.

3.**Lesser failure rate:**

Due to active involvement from users of the product, the validation of the idea and the functionality happens way ahead in the product development process. This ensures the products that are not useful to the user community are not taken up for development and hence reduces the risk of failed products. Even if the companies or OSH enthusiast moves out of a particular product, the development of that product can still be continued by others as all the required documents etc. are already made available to the OSH community. If a product is considered not useful, the idea and knowledge about that product or functionalities are available for application in other products and also can be taken up for further processing during a later date or circumstance when it is considered useful. In OSH world nothing goes waste. Even unpopular idea or design contributes in its own way. First thing is it will reduce the wastage of effort as users will not spend time on such unpopular ideas as they would look into the knowledge base before starting a new project. Second is, a product which is not popular in a particular situation, time frame, market, location, group etc. could become highly popular in a different set of situation, time frame, market etc. So the process which was put on hold due to a product not being popular can be restarted when it becomes popular.

4. **Can be applied to wide range of products:**

Even though ideas submitted are being developed as one single product, most of the OSH users look at it as a bundle of plug-and-play features. Many times new products are developed just by mix and match of different functionalities already available in different products. This might be due to the very nature of the OSH products being developed by using cheap components available in the market. So, once products are developed, the functionalities available in them are available to be used by wide variety of other products. This is very helpful for DIY projects or for products for social causes.

5. **Highly customize-able and configurable:**

As the design and other documents relating to a product are readily available to everyone, anyone can customize and configure them according to their requirement. This also makes repairing and upgrading easy and inexpensive as specific component can be replaced or upgraded. As mentioned earlier, many times new products are developed though mix and match of functionalities available in different products, which is achieved by combination of various OSH components. Extending this approach further, you can give the option of configuring a product to the user according to their requirements. Also, with on-demand and localized production you have the ability to customize color, shape, size, look and feel and other attributes as per user requirement.

6. **Reduces distribution and inventory costs:**

Due to the ability to manufacture on-demand and locally, OSH based product manufacturing reduces the cost of shipping from a central location to sellers across the world and also eliminates the requirement to stock the product in warehouses at different locations. The complexity in traditional manufacturing and distribution processes has led to highly complex logistics process, where as in OSH approach the process is maintained very simple. Either the products are manufactured by the OSH professionals themselves or they get it manufactured by local small scale producers to meet the local demands. This reduces the cost of the product to a great extent and also reduces the burden on a country to import huge quantities of oil and also reduce the adverse impact on environment.

7. **Can be used for social causes:**

As the products are very cheap and all the ideas are

available for application in any product, NGOs and other social organizations can utilize them for developing products that will help in social causes like safety, health and sanitation. Users who are looking to helping out on social cause can do mix and match of functionalities from current projects in a way that could cater to the social cause and then assemble them locally at a very low cost. NGOs and other organizations can provide new ideas to OSH community that could help in social cause, which then can be developed by volunteers willing to contribute to those social causes. High tech companies can use a part of their CSR budget towards developing new products for social causes as well.

Now let's take a look at disadvantages of OSH product development process.

1. **Low accountability and responsibility:**

Since the products are developed by many people through collaboration, accountability and responsibility of the final product may not be clearly laid out. This could lead to non-servicing of the product if any issues arise. Unless you are knowledgeable of the design of the product or there are sufficient help available it would be difficult to troubleshoot any issues. This could lead to lots of junks piling up as users might get into use-and-throw attitude.

2. **Chances of legal issues:**

Currently the same licensing option available for open source software is being applied for open source hardware as well, which may not be appropriate. Also, since many people would be contributing to the product, there are chances that some of them could use contents that violate IP laws. Junking sub-process could also lead to IP law violations. Since OSH community is well spread across the world they'll have to deal with laws in different countries. Some of the corporates could use ideas and products generated through OSH community and try to get patents and IP rights, which could lead to long and costly legal battles.

3. **Chances of lower quality:**

Since individuals will be using their own tools and equipment during tinkering and manufacturing they might be using sub-standard tools and equipment which could affect the quality of the product. Materials used could also be sub-standard due to unavailability or higher cost of good quality materials. There could also be hundreds of designs, components and products available online and in stores which would make it difficult to identify a good quality product that would meet the product requirements. As the design and other details are freely available, there could be chances of fake and counterfeit products with low quality being produced. It will be very difficult for consumers to identify a good quality product as there could be huge number of products available in the market.

4.**Usage by anti-social elements:**

Due to the free availability of the product design and easy manufacturing, it will be difficult to check the usage of the product. Hence there are chances that the product could be used by anti-social elements in illegal activities. These sects of people could mix and match the functionality of different product and come up with new products for using them in illegal or anti-social activities. It will be very difficult for local authorities to monitor this as the development could be done in isolation within houses, garages etc. The network of such anti-social elements could become very active online and collaborate in illegal activities across the world.

5.**High obsolescence rate:**

While accelerated product development and progressive releases bring in new products quicker, it could also lead to huge number of obsolescence. As a new product is released with better functionality, people will buy them and the older product will become obsolete. New releases of the same product could also lead to obsolescence of the earlier versions. This will lead to junkyards being piled up with obsolete products and if the junkyard is not managed well, could become a major issue for a community.

From the discussions in this chapter, you would now know about various advantages of OSH approach and hence make use of them in your product development process. As you now understand the disadvantages, you can plan for mitigating strategies to overcome them, in case issues arise in your project.

CHAPTER 6

OSH for DIY projects

Currently most of the products developed using open source approach are do it yourself (DIY) type of projects with the use of open source hardware components. This is an important entry point into OSH space and it could turn into critical stepping stone for future innovators. We have seen many live examples in history where in DIY type of projects have become commercially successful products and also introduced many disruptive technologies and new concepts. So, let's look at some basic concepts that could help readers to take up more and more DIY projects. These can be applied for other types of product development as well. It is also important to note at this point that in OSH space one of the main manufacturing options is for users to manufacture their own product using shared information and knowledge. This is similar to DIY projects, but all the information is readily available for the users. Once many more products are made available to users, there will be more and more people taking up OSH based manufacturing. This chapter would help such users to get basic understanding of OSH based DIY projects and then use them for manufacturing their own products. Below is a diagrammatic representation of how a simple OSH product would be configured.

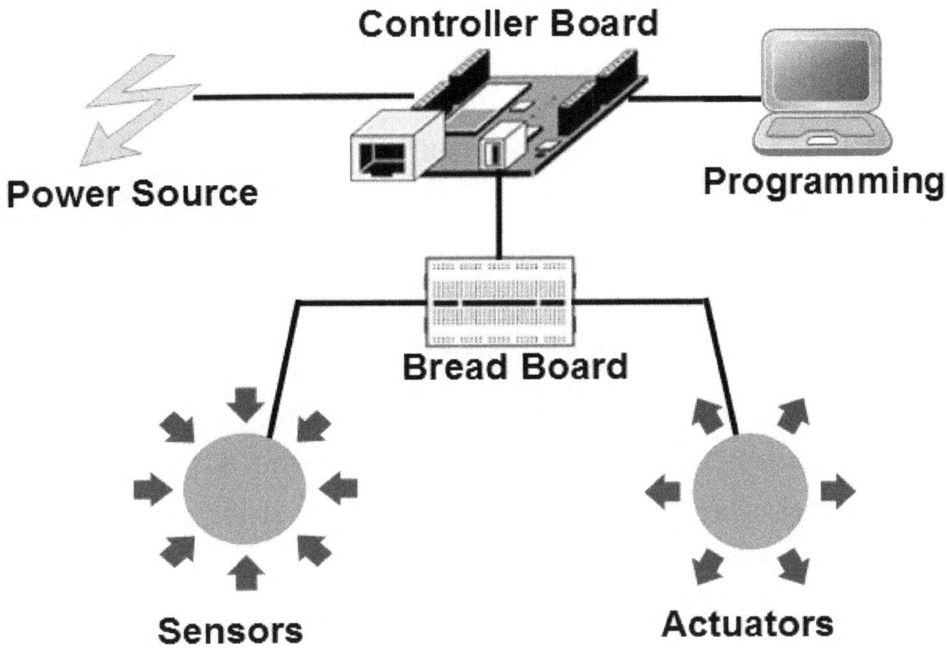

As you can see from the above diagram, the common components in an OSH project would be power source, microprocessor, programming, breadboard, sensors and actuators. Below are further details of each of these components.

1. **Power source:**

   All components need power input for their working. However, the volts and watts for each of them differ. Based on the requirement of these components appropriate power source need to be included in your project. Also, based on the functionality of the product, you need to decide whether direct plug in is required or battery option need to be included. There are options for including solar based power source as well.

2. **Microprocessor:**

This is the central processing unit of any product. All other components need to be connected to this central unit. It has different slots to connect the sensors and actuators. It also has slots for connecting to the power source and USB slot for connecting to an computer. Based on the readings received from sensors, instructions are sent to the actuators to act particular manner. Logic for this is provided through software codes written on desktops or laptops connected to these microprocessors and then uploaded into the board.

3. **Programming:**

The microprocessor can be programmed by connecting it to a desktop or laptop. Easy to use interfaces are provided by the vendors of the board, through which scripts can be developed for creating logic and functionality of the product. Once the program is tested by running it directly from the interface, it can be uploaded on to the board, for the product to work without connecting to an external system.

4. **Breadboard:**

This is the component used to connect various

components easily to microprocessor. It will not only make the connections to be placed in an organized manner but also to mix and match connections to multiple components without messing up the connections on the microprocessor. You can also place small components like switches, resistors etc. directly on the breadboard. This is of great help to DIY projects as you can play around with the connections easily. Without breadboard you'll have to make permanent connections using soldering tools and hence changing the configurations become very difficult. Also providing the connection details and design is much easier with a breadboard in picture, which will help users to easily follow these details and manufacture on their own without much effort. Extending or reducing the reach of a product by adding multiple sets of sensors and actuators becomes very easy with the use of breadboards.

5. **Sensors:**

These are components that read different measurements from outside world and feed them into the microprocessor. Sensors could be reading different measures like moisture, temperature or even visuals. Inputs could be analog or digital. The microprocessor will then process this data as per the requirement.

6. **Actuators:**

These are components that perform some action

based on instructions from the microprocessor. Usually the microprocessors read measurements and other data from the sensors and based on the reading send instructions to actuators to take actions. The actuators could be lights, fans, motors etc.

One of the other important things required for open source hardware product development is a good lab for you to work in. If you are into DIY, you'll probably have to build your own lab from scratch. Many institutions, corporates, government organizations or local community groups establish labs for public use to encourage DIY mindset and innovations. You can check if such labs exist in your locality and use them for your projects. Let's look at a typical lab setup used for DIY type projects.

1. **Furnishing:**

   You'll need a large and spacious lab table to work on. As you'll be doing lots of rough work it is better to have wooden or metal surface. It should be easy to clean as it could get dirty based on the type of projects you would take up. You'll also need a chair that is easy to sit as well as move around, may be something similar to bar stools with back rest. As you might spend a lot of time in the lab, seating needs to be comfortable. You could also have some sofas and other comfortable furnishing to be used while you are not working on the product but doing some reading, brainstorming, knowledge sharing, documenting etc. Providing TV and video conferencing facilities would be fun as well.

2. **Components:**

This is the raw material that goes into the product. While the requirement for the components depends on the product you are working on, many components are commonly used by most of the products. So, you can buy such components in bulk and stock them up for your current projects as well as for future projects. Usually, OSH enthusiasts work on multiple projects at a time and also try to come up with new projects by tinkering around with components they have. You can also look at buying component kits which work out cheaper. The common components regularly used are, different configurations of microprocessors, switches, LEDs, small motors, breadboards, light sensors, temperature sensors, distance sensors, motion sensors, cameras etc.

3. **Small parts:**

You'll need many small parts to assemble various components and other parts of the product. These are very commonly used parts not only for open source products but could be for any type of DIY projects. It could be nails and screws, threads and strings, stationary like glue, stapler, oil, bearings etc. As it is easier and cheaper to buy in bulk and as these parts need to be readily available while tinkering, it is better to stock them up in your labs.

4. **Laptop or tablet:**

You'll need to connect to internet very often for different reasons not only during idea generation or knowledge sharing but also during active tinkering. Designs, instructions etc. shared by others are referred constantly while the product is assembled or built. So, it's better to use a laptop or tablet as you can move it around the lab while you are on to different tasks. You'll need a webcam as well to interact with other users as well as record the issues, instructions etc. For programming also laptop or tablet would be useful as you need to test the code while connected to the microprocessor.

5. **Tools:**

Requirement of tools depend on the type of product you are developing. Simple tools like screw drivers, spanners or hammers could be sufficient for simple products. For others you might need soldering tools, drillers, saw, cutters, polishers etc. You might need different software tools for designing, documenting, recording etc.

6. **3D printer:**

If your product has some mechanical movement and you are not able to find cheap parts to develop it, you can use 3D printers for building those parts. You can use self-replicating printers like RepRap if you need mostly plastic parts. RepRap is cheap and you can get most of the parts printed from your friend's printer. If you need to print parts with other materials you can buy costlier printers those that have different print heads. You'll also have to stock the materials used by these printers.

7. **Junkyard:**

For DIY type of projects you try to re-use components from other electronic items. So, it would be helpful to build a junk yard with items that you don't use anymore or items that are not working but could have some good parts inside it. You can use these items to research some of the common electronic products by ripping open and analyzing how they work. You can either go through your junkyard periodically and dig out components that you might need or based on you product requirement you can fish out specific components from them.

8. **Safety equipment:**

As you'll be doing lot of rough work and using some tools to assemble the products, it is better to use safety equipment while working on your products. These could be as simple as gloves, safety glasses, apron, masks, shoes etc. It is also better to keep fire extinguishers as well as to make the lab child proof. You might also want to add safety equipment in your electrical connections to avoid any issues relating to electricity.

9. **Testing equipment:**

For DIY type of projects it will be difficult to get the products tested professionally and hence it would be good to build your own testing lab using cheap testing equipment. You could probably build a small temperature controlled chamber for testing temperature attributes, small water tanks, small fire chamber, small wind tunnel etc. With this you can probably be able to provide some testing services to other OSH enthusiasts.

From the above details it should be clear as to how typical DIY type of projects work and also how you can setup your own lab for taking up OSH based DIY projects. Having good understanding of basic concepts provided in this chapter will also help in easy walk through of the case study provided in the next chapter. You can also refer back to this chapter in case you realize that some of the concepts are not yet clear.

CHAPTER 7

Case Study 1

In this chapter we will take up a hypothetical example as case study so that readers can get a walk-through of a practical implementation of the OSH product development process. It is suggested that the readers refer to the chapter on product development process for the theoretical aspect and then come back to this chapter to understand more from practical implementation point of view. This chapter becomes a very good reference point while they are developing a product to get some practical tips and guidance. This chapter is built around a character named James who is a OSH enthusiast and trying to develop a product for his own use through OSH approach. James' requirement is to build an automated home garden using OSH products. This is probably a popular requirement for many double income families staying in major cities, who do not have free time during weekdays to maintain a garden, but would like to reap the benefits of having own garden. The sections are same as the steps mentioned in the product development process for OSH and hence it is easy to understand and refer back to that chapter. Even though James is not a real life character, the case study has been documented as realistic as possible to help the readers to get the experience of a practical experience.

1. **Idea Generation:**

This is a new idea generated based on the requirements of James. Due to the current health concerns emerging because of the practices followed by growers and traders, James would like to go for organically grown vegetables and fruits. However, the organic farm products available in the market are costly, not fresh and may not be truly organic. So James wants to grow his own organic vegetables and fruits. Due to space constraints, he would like to setup a garden in the balcony of the apartment. Also to reduce the effort and to make it efficient he would like to automate the functioning of the garden. The automation is required for day-to-day maintenance of the garden and tasks that needs to be taken up once in a while. So the two areas that require automation are:

1. Watering, temperature control and lighting adjustment
2. Reaping, fertilizing and weeding

As a first step, James would search online if someone has already shared similar idea and check if it meets his requirements. If available he will provide his feedback to further fine tuning the idea or the product according to his requirement. If not available, James will share the idea with OSH community for comments and feedback from them. Currently, there is no single website where you can find details about all the OSH projects. You'll have to search different sites to get this information, including various forums and blogs. There are groups in social networking sites that share information on OSH products. You'll have to put in considerable effort in searching and posting your requirements. James has been interested in OSH for long time and hence pretty updated on where to look out and also post. Based on this experience he has searched and posted information of his idea to build an automated garden. James has received multiple feedback and many of them also have shown keen interest in the product. Some of them even have directed James to places where he can find products that have some of the functionalities he is looking for, which he can do a mix and match to his product. James is already excited with the power of collaboration and is looking forward to see his product becoming a reality.

2. **Shared Knowledge:**

There are details of multiple OSH based products shared online. Many times you'll be able to assemble and configure your own product by mixing and matching features of different products. Based on the research of this knowledge base and with the help of other OSH users, James is able to further fine-tune the requirement and build a high level design of his product. For easy reference and for further processing, let's divide the product into two parts:

1. Daily maintenance – for watering, maintaining temperature, lighting controls

2. On-demand maintenance – for reaping, fertilizing and weeding

Below is the high level design description James is able to put together based on his research and help from others. Each of the above will have an input, processing and action. For daily maintenance the inputs will be moisture level, temperature of the air, illumination level. The measure from these inputs needs to be processed and checked if they are within a range. Action needs to be taken if it's not within the range. Action here would be to dispense water, operate the cooler or heater and control the lighting. For on-demand maintenance, inputs would be mainly visual, processing would be done by interpreting the visuals and matching it with predefined criteria. The visuals could be relayed through online tools for processing by the user manually. The action here is more of physical in nature, like plucking and storing the produce as well as removing the unwanted growths.

This is good progress in terms of taking the initial idea to a detailed requirement and high level design based on shared knowledge available online. Since OSH is based on collaboration and shared knowledge, James would share the consolidated information back on to the OSH websites. This will not only help others who have similar requirement but he will also get feedback from other OSH enthusiasts, which will help James to further fine-tune his requirements. Now, James is not only excited with the power of collaboration but also able to see how accelerated product development is happening due to that. On his own he would not have been able to progress so fast in finalizing the idea and coming up with high level design.

3. **Components:**

Based on the inputs, processing and actions listed down in earlier steps, OSH components need to be identified. First let's look at the requirement of components for the processing part. The obvious component choice for processing task in OSH products would be Arduino, as it is cheap, easy to configure and highly programmable. We will use the latest available version which is UNO R3 board. Next let's take a look at components required for input section. Based on the online research for moisture level check, simple metal screws can be used. Cheap thermistor components are also available for checking the temperature. Simple photocell components can be used for sensing light level. Video component like Pixy is required for visual input. Components required for actions would be small water pump, humidifier, fans, heater, led lights, couple of motors. You'll also need power source and units, breadboards for arranging the components, resistors, wires, pipes, water storage etc. You'll also need parts for assembling and packaging these components. For physical movements, parts like wheels, gears, strings, rods etc. are also required. Many times you might have to come back to this process as you progress with the product development and if you need to make any modifications in the design or functionality. James has now identified all the components and parts, and listed them out including the quantities and ready for the next step. He is again able to use collaboration to identify best components by posting questions on blogs and other forums.

4. **Tinkering:**

Once the components are identified we also need to identify how to procure them. Some of them you need to buy and few others you might be able to get through junking process. These components are available at very cheap rates on some of the online stores as well as in local electronics components shops. Some vendors even sell it as kits which include most of the common components required for building common OSH products. Before you buy any of the components you have to go through few more steps in tinkering process to check if you can get those components through other methods. Let's look at the sub processes within the tinkering process.

Junking: In this process let's check for components and parts that we can reuse by opening up household unused items. Some of the common components and parts you can get by junking are motors, pumps, power supplies, wires, pipes, storage containers, fans, heaters, led lights, Wi-Fi enablers etc. Common source would be electronic toys, consumer durable items, gadgets, computer and cell phone accessories. Junk plastic and metal items can also be fished out for other parts that might be required for storage or mechanical and physical actions. James is able to find most of the items required under the 'action' category of the project through junking process. He has updated the list of components and parts to mark which of the identified components and parts are available now through the junking process. He is very happy that he is able to make good use of old unused items and also how he is able to reduce the cost of the project through this process.

3D Printing: Non-electronics components can be developed through 3D printing. Currently only plastic print heads are available through OSH based 3D printers. Mechanical parts like gears, hooks, wheels etc. can be easily printed through these 3D printers. As lots of physical movement is required for actions to be performed in on-demand maintenance unit of the project, James decided to build the parts through 3D printing. James was able to get most parts of the self-replicating 3D printer RepRap through a friend who already has a working RepRap printer. He bought the remaining parts of the printer on an online store and then easily assembled his own 3D printer. Designs for most common parts are available online as well, which can be downloaded and used to print those parts. James was able to research and find design for mechanical movements through OSH websites and then he identified the parts required for those designs. He was also able to get RepRap compatible designs for those parts and then print the parts very easily. After this he has updated the components and parts list to mark the parts he has printed. Remaining components and parts that he could not get by junking or printing he has purchased at a local electronics shop. This whole experience has given James a lot of intellectual and innovation satisfaction. He would have never imagined that he would have experienced these new areas and create products using 3D printers. He is feeling very thankful to the OSH community as only through collaboration and knowledge sharing this was possible.

Assembling: In this phase all the components and parts that are purchased, junked, printed are put together as a product. This is the first chance to check if all the components and parts are working. In the garden project the components relating to daily maintenance unit will be mostly stationed at one position and may not be moved regularly. However, inputs are required from wide area and action needs to be applied to a wide area as well. So, there will be multiple sets of same components placed at different areas in the garden. These components need to be connected through breadboards to the central microprocessor. The input components should also be easily mapped to the action components as action needs to be taken in a specific section of the garden based on the measurement coming through input components in that section. For on-demand maintenance unit there will be very less electronics components and many mechanical parts. The central unit will have the microprocessor, pixy components and many motors. It will be connected through strings, gears, wheels, pipes etc. for moving around the garden. Action will be taken through mechanical arms, suction cups etc. All these components will be assembled and initial checking done. Any issues faced will have to be resolved before getting into next phase. Soldering tool, screw drivers, drilling machine, spanners, saw, hammer, wrench, lots of screws, nuts and bolts were used for assembling. James has assembled both the sections and also packaged them using some plastic boxes and containers. He has also verified if all of the components are working by connecting them separately to power units and performed any adjustments required. The excitement is growing further for James as he is now able to see his product taking shape so fast and almost ready for usage.

Programming: Nice thing about OSH based products is that most of the functionality can be easily built through programming, which is one of many reason for increasing popularity of OSH based product development and DIY projects. The Arduino board can be plugged into a desktop or a laptop through an USB cable. Arduino provides a programming tool that can be installed on your desktop and can be used for writing easy scripts. Many scripts are also available online which can be downloaded and modified according to your requirements. For the garden project, we need two sets of programming one for the board used in the daily maintenance unit and the other for the board in on-demand maintenance unit. For daily maintenance we need a program to read the measurements from input components, check if they are within a range and take action accordingly. Let's break this down further

– The program should check the moisture level through the components installed for measuring the soil moisture. If the measurement shows the soil is dry, the water pump should be switched on and water directed to appropriate section of the garden which is dry.

– The program should check the temperature from thermistor components attached to the board. If the temperature is high, fan and humidifier needs to be switched on. If its low, heater and fans need to be switched on.

– The program needs to check the light level through the photocell component attached to the board. If its too dark during day time, the lights need to be switched on. If its too sunny then appropriate shades needs to be activated.

Programming for on-demand unit would be a bit complex as it will require image processing as well as Wi-Fi access to do remote controlling of the unit. Below are further details of the programming requirements.

– The program should be able to move the unit across the whole garden on a periodic basis and capture the video of the plants and produce, using the Pixy component. The board should read the video captured from the Pixy component and compare it to predefined image criteria, which would indicate whether the produce is ready for reaping or not. If the criterion matches, the mechanical arms should be able to pluck it and move it into a storage unit.

– Similar to the above requirement, the program

should be able to identify weeds based on image comparison and then pluck them out.

– The program should be able to direct the mechanical arms to disperse fertilizer during predefined time intervals at predefined locations.

– The program should be able to stream the video through Wi-Fi to a local system and then over the internet to any location, so that the garden can be monitored easily without being present physically at the location.

– A client software is required that can send instructions to the on-demand maintenance unit to take actions as per the instructions provided by the user remotely, for any events that is not automated and requires manual intervention.

After extensive search James is able to find programs for pixy component, robotic arms, Wi-Fi connections etc. He is continuing his search of programs for live streaming over the internet and also for controlling the unit remotely. In case of unavailability he'll place a request online for the same with OSH community. James has modified the code according to his requirement for all the features, has done a quick check by connecting to the boards and uploading them on to the boards. This is the best part in any innovator's or product developer's life, where in they are able to see a fully working output of their effort and James is also enjoying this part of his life.

5. **Prototyping**:

Once you have assembled and programmed, you need to test it out in live environment. Sometimes you might have to simulate or do a lab test of different conditions as you may not be able to find all conditions in a selected live environment. Apart from installing and testing in his own garden, James will use the product in the gardens of friends and family to check any installation issues and also to get useful user feedback. James has also asked his teammates to setup new gardens and use the product so as to get feedback from different sets of users who could look at the product from a completely different perspective. He has also contacted some of the OSH enthusiasts who are already using some simple automation tools currently, and asked them to use this product and provide their feedback. James uses some household utilities for packaging the product so that it becomes a bit user friendly, enhances the look and feel, and helps in shipping and installing at his friends and team mates gardens. He also creates a user guide that can be used by the prototype testers for installing, configuring and daily usage of the product. James puts together a list of different conditions that needs to be tested and identifies which conditions require simulation or lab tests and sends the details of remaining conditions to the testers so that they can provide the results back to

James later.

Below are some of the issues and feedback he gets from the users, which he plans to address in the next versions of the prototypes or the product itself.

1. As the range of measurement differs based on the crop, option needs to be provided for users to change it according to the crop they'll be planting.

2. Central units need to be covered in material which is weather proof as the garden could be exposed to different conditions.

3. As different users could have different sizes of gardens, option for reduction and expansion of the application area and component sets of the product is required.

4. Option for choosing between ground based or string based on-demand maintenance unit is required, so that it can moved around based on the layout of the garden.

5. Plant cutting options need to be added along with plucking options in the robotic arms for reducing the damage on the soft produce.

6. Different types of irrigation options like drip, sprinklers, gravity based, to be provided rather than just pump based direct watering.

7. Suggestions were also provided on packaging and installation guides to make it look professional

and easy to use.

The major change required was to provide configuring ability to the user. So, instead of hard coding some of the values, James changed the program to read the values from a file. Option was provided for the user to update this file according to their requirement and upload it to the board. This would take care of many of the feedback received. James plans to provide touch screen based configuring option in future versions of the product. Other defects and issues noted during the prototype testing were also fixed. The product has already become a great hit among urban families who have been closely monitoring the progress of the product. Many OSH enthusiasts and professionals are also reviewing the feedback and issues reported by the testers and actively participating in resolving them. This has been a very unique and enjoyable experience for James.

6. **Manufacturing**:

First thing to be done in this phase is to share all the details of the product with OSH community, so that not only they can manufacture it for their usage, but can do further incremental development on the product. So, James will upload not only the design, assembly instructions, programs and user guides but also a detailed video with all the instructions. There are different types of manufacturing options available and depending on the demand appropriate option needs be selected.

– Small scale home based manufacturing may not require much investment but the production process used will have higher per unit production cost. When you don't have clear picture on the demand or the demand is small and localized, this would be the safest and best option. In this option you could go for cost plus pricing for your product.

– When you have moderate demand or seasonal product, you could go for medium scale manufacturing option. The investment would be a bit higher but the per unit production cost would be lower. Also, you have the liberty to use creative pricing option, which could be higher than cost plus price.

– In large scale production, investment would be highest but the cost of product would be the lowest. This is the most preferred option for traditional product development and manufacturing process.

The preferred option for OSH based product development would be the small scale production, which would enable collaboration, knowledge sharing, incremental development, on-demand, flexible and localized production. There are efforts going on to bring in new technologies and processes to reduce the per unit production cost in small scale production option without increasing the investment. James would go for the small scale production option as it is appropriate for his situation. He has started marketing the product through various free websites as well as created his own website using free hosting option. All the social networking sites are used to the fullest extent for making the user community aware of the product. He has also tied up with many OSH enthusiasts at different locations for marketing, manufacturing and shipping the product depending on the shipping location of the order. Orders have started trickling in and he is able to use the small profit to implement his other ideas and also to contribute to ideas from other enthusiasts. He is also in discussions with local manufacturers to explore flexible manufacturing options in case the demand increases or if he gets a large order.

7. **<u>Consumers or users:</u>**

Many times the product developed through tinkering process itself could reach the users as a full-fledged product. However, if a manufacturing option is selected, the product could be moving to users after it is produced by the manufacturer. Users may also use the shared information of the product to produce it on their own. This would allow them to configure and customize the product according to their requirement. In OSH based product development consumers or users will have a major role in various aspects of the product development.

Their involvement would start from the idea generation stage itself and continues even after product is manufactured and shipped. For the garden project, James received many feedbacks at various stages of the development from the users. The new idea posted online was reviewed by many users and useful feedback received by them. James was able to adjust his idea accordingly which ensured the downstream processes of design and implementations also took care of those feedback. Even though James selected only few of the users for prototype testing, many had downloaded the information shared and provided useful feedback which James implemented in the final product. Users are already providing new ideas for next version of the product and many of them have already started doing incremental improvements to the products, on their own.

As you can see from the above case study, James who was a novice in electronic product development was able to easily develop a product as per his requirement very quickly and with very low cost. This would have not been possible with traditional approach. The structured OSH product development process documented in this book also helped James to utilize the benefits of OSH approach easily. He is also able to realize the power of collaboration and shared knowledge and feeling very satisfied with the overall experience. James is now all pumped up to take up more product development and is also helping others by contributing to their product development. He has put together a detailed release plan for the next versions in collaboration with other OSH enthusiasts who have already started working on new features to his product. Let us hope that each reader gets encouraged with the experience of James, sees a James within themselves and takes on active participation in OSH product development.

Case studies in different areas will be looked into, documented and released to the readers in future. James will be contributing in various areas and picking up new skills as well as experience. Readers are suggested to check out for these new case studies and grow along with James in the area of open source hardware product development.

CHAPTER 8

OSH Components and tools

Components are very important part of OSH products. It's important to understand different types of components available in the market so that you are aware of which components to use in your products. The components could be relating to sensors that can be used to get inputs from the external environment, microprocessors that can be used for processing the measurement received from the sensors and send instructions to other components, actuators that perform some specific actions based on the instructions received. There could be other components like batteries, power units, breadboards, resistors, capacitors etc. Tools are anything that would be used during the tinkering or manufacturing process. 3D printers, screwdrivers, soldering tools, drills etc. are tools commonly used during the tinkering process.

Let's look at these components and tools in detail here as this could help the readers to easily look out for these components for their products and tools to be used during tinkering process.

1. **Microprocessors:**

Microprocessors are small circuit boards having computing capability. They usually read data from different sensors connected to them, process the data and then instruct the actuators to take actions. They can be connected to your laptops or desktop through USB port and upload programming scripts that are coded according to the requirement or functionality to be made available in your product. A huge number of microprocessors are available with different capability, capacity and functionalities. So you need to analyze as to what type of processor is required for your product and then match it with what's available in the market. There are many microprocessors that are developed using OSH approach and hence are available for very low price. This is one area where lots of new product development is happening and hence huge advances are expected in future.

2. **Sensors**:

   1. Cameras

      They are also called image or vision sensors. The main functionality is to capture the images and then transmit them to the microprocessors. New components available under OSH come with functionality to identify objects and can be programmed to take actions upon detection of an object.

2. Humidity sensors:

Humidity is the amount of water in the air. Controlling or monitoring humidity is required for many purposes, especially for industries, agriculture etc. You can use humidity sensors for this purpose as they indicate moisture levels in the environment.

3. Motion sensors:

You might need functionality in your product for taking some action based on any physical movement. Motion sensors detect any physical movement happening within a given range. You can connect these to your microprocessor and program it to identify any motion.

4. Audio sensors:

Audio sensors can detect presence of sound within a range. They can not only send information to microprocessor when a sound is present but they can also provide the amplitude or strength details.

5. Bio-metrics:

There are different types of bio-metrics sensors available in the market. These are used to capture different attributes from humans or animals. Very common ones are finger print scanners and retina scanners, which are used for identification purpose. New components like pulse sensors, heart rate monitors have also been introduced recently.

6. Light sensors:

Light sensors convert the light energy, whether visible or infrared format, into an electrical output. You can use these sensors not only to detect if there is light or not, but amount of light as well. Infrared light sensors could be used for advance functionality in environments that do not or cannot have normal lighting.

7. Temperature sensors:

Commonly used temperature sensor is called thermistor which can give the measurement of heat. You'll have to do some adjustments in your program as each thermistor will have some resistance values depending on the material used in the component. This component is becoming very common in wearable products and health-care products.

8. Touch sensors:

Touch sensors come with different functionalities. It could be simple touch sensing buttons or switches to full-fledged touch based user interface components. Instead of providing mechanical buttons and switches you can go for touch sensing buttons or switches in your product as they are more durable and have better look and feel, usability attribute. In the same manner, you can provide some functionality where in users can use a touch screen to interact with your product instead of having to connect to their systems for such instructions.

3. **Actuators**:

1. Heating and cooling:

Any simple heating and cooling components can be used for temperature related actions. If the temperature is high as per the temperature sensor, you can switch on the cooler and if the temperature is low, you can switch on the heater. The microprocessor could be programmed to handle this automatically. Each of them has a capacity and range. You need to analyze the requirement of your product and identify the right type of heater or cooler.

2. Audio and Video:

Any audio or video components can be connected to the OSH microprocessors. Mics, speakers, LCD displays are the common audio and video components and these days they are becoming portable. Many of them are being made Wi-Fi or Bluetooth enabled and hence you'll need to include a Wi-Fi or Bluetooth connector through which these components can be connected remotely.

3. LED and lights:

One of the common components used in most of the OSH product is LED or other types of lights. You can directly connect them to the breadboard itself or to an external connector. You can also make display boards etc. using a series of LED bulbs and then programming to display different messages. They not only use very less electricity but are also very durable.

4. Motors:

For most of the mechanical movements you'll need motors. They are available in different capacity and you have to select the right one based on your requirement. Motors need power input and hence you have to include appropriate power source for them. Some products require very small motors to be placed at different places to provide very delicate movements. Very powerful motors are used for heavy duty tasks.

4. **Other components:**

1. Batteries

Batteries are the most common power source used in OSH products. The advantage of using a battery is, the product can be made portable as it need not be connected to a fixed power line. Using rechargeable batteries will reduce the maintenance cost of the product. The battery strength will again be determined based on the power requirement of your product. You can also add in solar or other rechargeable components so that the product becomes self-sustainable.

2. Power units

If you have to connect your product to an external power source, you might need a separate power unit to be attached to the product. To make it a global product, you would have to add converters so that it can work in different countries that have different power requirements. Many countries required power units to be certified due to safety reasons. Hence it is better to look at these requirements and ensure you select the right components.

3. Breadboards

This component helps in easily connecting other components to the microprocessor without soldering. It is mainly used during tinkering and prototyping phases so that you can move the connections around easily. It also keeps the connections very well arranged and reduces mess. Once the product is finalized, the connections are removed from breadboard and connected permanently through soldering so that they don't get disconnected during the usage of the product.

4. Resistors

If you have a component that needs lesser electrical current than available through the power source, you can use resistors. Resistors are made out of materials that reduce the electrical current. The resistors are color coded so that users can easily identify the resistance and tolerance.

5. Capacitors

Capacitors are components that can store small amounts of energy. There are different types of capacitors used for different purpose. So, you need to understand these capacitors to know which one to use in your product. It could be used for smooth electrical supply, filtering noise, brief energy storage and supply etc.

5. **<u>Tools</u>**:

1. 3D printers

3D printers are becoming an essential part of any OSH lab. There are simple and cheap 3D printers that can print only plastic materials. Costlier and sophisticated printers can print using different materials and also complex designs. They could also be using different methods to bind these materials. Depending on your requirements you could buy an appropriate printer.

2. Screwdrivers and spanners

These are some of the simplest tools that you could be using on a day-to-day basis in your garage. You'll need them for OSH products during the assembling process. Again depending on your product requirements you might have to buy these with different sizes and ranges. Battery operated options are also available.

3. Drills

Many times you might have to drill holes in parts that you use for your products. Especially when you do junking and use materials from junkyards, drilling might be required. Wooden or metal parts might also require holes to fix them to other components. You can go for either manual drills or power drilling machines.

4. Soldering tools

Most of the components have metal components and needs to be fixed permanently. Soldering tools help you in doing this permanent connection between components. Soldering might be required for other metal parts as well. For bigger parts you might have to go for welding machines for connecting them.

The components and tools discussed in this chapter are mainly used for creating DIY projects of small OSH products. For complex products you might need other complex components and tools. The list is expected to grow very rapidly in near future as new components are invented and made available for usage.

CHAPTER 9

Licensing

Traditionally products have been registered for patenting, intellectual property rights or copyrights and then different licenses provided from the rights holders to the users or manufacturers of the product. Digital or other materials are subjected to copyrights and the physical product itself undergoes patenting or intellectual property rights. License is a way to give rights to others for something on which you have copyright or patent and intellectual property right, so that you can control how they are used and also to charge them accordingly. If there is no copyright or patent then everything is free and you don't need a license. In open source world the approach needs to be different as the concept is to open up the design and other items which are traditionally protected through patenting or copyright. Open source software is in existence for some time now and licensing for them is pretty advanced. So, open source hardware professionals are also trying to implement the concepts from open source software to open source hardware. However, the licensing methods used for software does not completely fit the requirements of hardware. There are efforts to develop a completely new set of licensing for open source hardware but they are still in initial stage and need considerable time and effort before it can be implemented. Also there is no regulatory body for making any rules or laws relating to open source hardware and hence there is no central custodian for this matter. Currently its being handled by an non-profit organization formed by volunteers from OSH space. There are still lots of confusion and discussions going on as to what all you need to share to claim a product as open source hardware.

open source hardware

First thing you need to do is place open source hardware logo on to your product as well all related material. This will ensure that everybody knows that your product is an open source hardware. Second thing you need to check is the OSHWA site to understand what are the various details and files you need to share to claim your product as open source hardware. Third thing you need to understand is different types of open source hardware licensing options available, select the appropriate one for your product and mention the license option you have selected in all the necessary locations. By doing this, users will know not only that your product is open source hardware but also what type of licensing you have selected and then follow all the requirements of that licensing option. Once you have selected and mentioned the license type in your product and materials, you also need to share all the required information as suggested by OSHWA.

Below are details of current licensing options for open source hardware:

1) **Copyleft** – licenses that require the upgrades or modified versions to have same license as the original product is called copyleft licenses. Some of the common licensing methods that fall under copyleft are GNU GPL, Creative Commons ShareALike, Open Hardware License etc. Let's look at some of these in detail.

   a) GNU GPL: This is an open source software related licensing that is being adapted to open source hardware. This license guarantees the end users freedom to share, study, use and modify the materials. Since this is a copyleft license, the derived works can only be distributed under the same license terms.

   b) Creative Commons – ShareALike: With this license, you can use, modify and build your own products but you need to provide credits to the original creator and then provide same license as the original license.

   c) Open Hardware License (OHL): There are two OHLs, CERN OHL and TARP OHL. CERN OHL governs how you use, copy, modify and distribute hardware design documents, and how you manufacture and distribute the products. TARP OHL is a framework, which is designed to guarantee the freedom to share and create, by forbidding denial of rights to copy, modify and distribute the documentation as well as to use, make and distribute products which are produced using the documentation.

2) **Permissive** – licenses that allow the upgrades or modified version to have their own licensing methods are called permissive licenses. FreeBSD, MIT license, Creative Commons Attribution licenses fall under this category.

a) FreeBSD: This is again a licensing used for open source software that is adapted to open source hardware. It's a family of permissive free licenses, named BSD licenses, which imposes minimal restriction on re-distribution of the documentation or the product manufactured there in.

b) MIT License: This is also an adaptation from open source software licensing, where in anyone who gets a copy of the documentation is free to use, copy, modify, merge, publish etc. It only requires a disclaimer to be provided in the licensing text.

c) Creative Commons – Attribution Licenses: This is one of the creative commons set of licenses that has minimal restriction which can be used for maximum dissemination and use of licensed materials. This license allows free distribution, modifications, re-build of materials and products there in, even commercially, with credits given to the original creator of the documentation and the product.

Licenses that do not allow commercial use of the design and other documents relating to the hardware are not considered as open source licenses.

So, if you want people to use the same license as yours, select one of the copyleft types of open source licenses for your product. In case you want to give free hand to people who use your product and other materials, you can go for permissive license type.

CHAPTER 10

Funding for OSH products

DIY type of projects or products that are made by assembling various OSH components do not need much funding. Not only are the raw materials for these products very cheap, but the consumers are usually ready to pay in advance for the product which can be used for funding. Major funding is required for complex projects or products and also for developing new types of OSH based sensors, microprocessors and actuators. Traditional way of funding is still available for even open source hardware products. Also there are companies that manufacture open source hardware or have open source hardware in their catalog, who will continue to fund and develop open source hardware. In this chapter we will mainly touch upon some of the traditional ways of funding product development. There are some new funding processes that are emerging these days and which is giving a boost to open source hardware product development. We will take a look at those funding methods as well.

Traditional methods of funding could be:

1. **Venture capital and Angel Investment:**

There are organizations and individuals who would like to invest in new ideas or ventures. They invest cash for a certain percentage of shares in the venture. This requires a thorough valuation of the venture as only intangible assets would have been generated till this stage in product development. The advantage of going with venture capitalists is that apart from cash, you get to tap the huge expertise they have in the area of business planning, marketing, finance etc. It is usually difficult to get a venture capitalist involved in a project as you'll need a very good story-line to invoke their interest. Usually 9 out of 10 ventures invested by venture capitalists fail, but they make it up with the one that becomes successful. Hence they are very skeptical about any new venture and need to be convinced about the feasibility and success factor of the project before they invest. OSH based ventures is a mixed bag for venture capitals. As there are quiet good feedback and involvement of users from the beginning of the product development process, you can easily make out the market demand etc. and hence it is easier to do a realistic valuation, where by risk of failure would be lower. However, since the design and other product details are available to everyone, anyone can manufacture and sell the product, which reduces the chances of making huge profits. So, you'll usually need a different type of story-line to get these venture capitalists to get involved in your venture.

2. **Organic financing:**

If you are working for a company that has internal funds allocated for new product development, you can use it for the purpose of your product development. Usually companies encourage IP or patent based product development, so you'll have to check if OSH based products are inline with the company objectives and build a business case accordingly. If your product would help in any social causes, you might be able to tap into funds allocated to CSR activities as well. Companies will usually require various forms to be filled up along with financial details and will require approvals from senior management. So it would be beneficial if you keep all the details ready as well as socialize your idea and products with various people from senior management. You can also present your idea or product in internal and external contests which can get you good visibility as well as easy funding.

3. **Grants**:

Governments and different organization earmark funds for promoting specific areas of their interest. They would also be ready to provide these funds as grants for projects that meet or promote their objectives. They usually work through different agencies to identify and shortlist such projects. Once you have finalized on your new idea, you can check out if it can be taken up as a project under any initiative and can get the grant funds for product development. If you are positive that your project meets the requirements of the initiative, you can reach out to the concerned agency and start the discussions. You can also explore the possibilities of making some modifications to your project so that it can meet the requirements of the initiative.

4. **Loans**:

Various banks and institutions also provide loans for new projects. It's a bit riskier proposition as you'll have to repay the loan as well as interest, no matter what happens with your product. You might have to give personal security or some asset as collateral security to the banks to get the loan. The advantage of going for loan is you'll not have any interference from others in your project as you'll have 100% stake or ownership and in case your project is a success, you don't need to share the benefits with others. Apart from loans taken from banks, you can also look at other debt instruments available in the market. You can also pursue debts from companies interested in your project with an option to convert them to equity at a later date.

5. **Equity**:

If you have a long term business plan or multiple ideas and products with multi-year development and release plan, then you can go for establishing a company and offer equity shares to the public to get the required funding. In case you already have a company you can issue additional shares for funding your new products. You can use equity to payout people who are contributing full time towards the product development. Issuing equity to people who are directly involved in product development will increase the sense of ownership and hence will secure their commitment towards the work.

6. **Bootstrapping**:

   When entrepreneurs use their own funds for new products or company, it's called bootstrapping. As the funds that an entrepreneur can raise on their own are limited, this type of funding is applicable where the funds required are low. Since the fund requirement for OSH based product development is very low, bootstrapping becomes a very good candidate for OSH approach. Also, the control stays with the entrepreneur, which is very much required for OSH based product development, where in the emphasis is on collaboration and sharing and not really on making huge profits.

New funding methods could be:

1. **Crowd-funding:**

   This is a new phenomenon in funding arena and its

getting very popular due to the capability to do online campaigning and funding options. When you have a new idea and would like to get some funding for taking the idea all the way to making it an usable product, you could launch a campaign on these websites. You need to come up with a price for the product and provide full details of your idea or product. You also need to set a time-line for the campaign as well as mention the minimum amount you want to raise out of the campaign. Based on how good your product is, the pricing, the market etc. interested buyers will start funding your campaign. You can use this money for product development process and then as per the time-lines mentioned you'll have to ship the finished product to people who have funded your campaign. You'll have to keep them updated regularly on the status of product development till the product is shipped. The crowd-funding website will charge a percentage as processing fees. Many innovators who are developing complex OSH products or new components for usage in OSH products are going for crowd-funding option as it creates a ready market along with providing required funding.

2. **Funding during 'Bridge of Death':**

A phenomenon applicable to crowd-funding is called 'bridge of death'. After the products pertaining to the pre-orders are shipped, there is a period when there is no demand for the product and hence the product could fail due to the lack of demand. This phenomenon is called bridge of death. Funding is required to sustain this low-demand period and also to create demand and build a scale-able, sustainable production process. There are new organizations getting into this space to ensure products or companies don't fail during this period and are converted to successful organizations.

We have discussed about traditional as well as new funding methods in this chapter. Even though you are currently looking at doing some DIY type of projects, it is always good to understand more about funding mechanisms as you never know when you could get a great idea and need to get into full-fledged product development. Also, if you have good savings, you could get into financing other interesting projects.

CHAPTER 11

Best Practices

As in any other process, one of the important steps in OSH process is to look at some of the best practices followed by different stakeholders and try to implement them. Since OSH product development is a new area, not many best practices available yet. Open Source Hardware Association is trying to come up with a list of best practices. On their site they have given a set of best practices that can be followed by OSH product developers. These include practices to be followed mainly around what needs to be shared regarding your product so that it could help others and some of the process and practices you need to follow during product development itself. Let's take a different approach in this book, by categorizing and then listing out the best practices in each of those categories. We have very good experience with bringing in best practices in the software world and also very knowledgeable on process improvements in ISO, CMM and other important standards. Based on this experience as well as additional research of best practices in OSH process we have come up with few categories for best practices and also included some best practices in each of these areas. As the process settles down in future, further research is required in collaboration with other individuals and organizations in coming up with a detailed documentation of best practices in OSH product development process. The main categories for best practices that is discussed in this chapter are standardize, simplify, reuse, modular and document. Let's look at each of these sections in detail.

1. **Standardize:**

   As in any process, standardization brings in a lot of efficiency and effectiveness. This is even more important in OSH space due to heavy dependency on collaboration and knowledge sharing. To ensure that various teams with different skill-sets and experience that are working on a project are all on the same page standardization is very important. Without standardizing, confusion could creep in and also could lead to effort and resource wastage. Standardization is required in all the steps of the product development. Templates need to be developed for filling in details of new idea generated, high level designs, component details, sketches, program codes, instructions etc. The whole process of product development itself also needs to be standardized. OSHWA has provide a list of documents, files and other resource that needs to be shared for a product to be considered truly 'open source'.

2. **Simplify:**

This is also a very important practice to be followed especially since the main reason for renewed focus on OSH is the ease of use and ease of building new products. To keep this trend going and to accelerate, product developers and contributors need to follow practices that will simplify the product and related materials. This is becoming even more important as many consumers themselves are taking up product manufacturing or assembly and non-engineers are getting more and more involved in new product development. One of the main areas that need to be very simple is how users configure or assemble the product. The users should be able to go through very simple instructions and then with very few steps and very few tools should be able to assemble the product. This is also important for the users to maintain the product on their own.

3. **Reuse:**

To reduce the effort and resources spent on product development, OSH product developers should follow a practice of reusing existing stuff instead of starting everything from scratch. Not only they need to look out for items that can be reused like designs, components, codes etc., but they also need to ensure that their products are developed in such a way that parts of it can be reused in other products by anyone. Also, due to availability of cheap OSH products, due to introduction of new products in rapid time-lines and due to faster obsolescence of a product there is a possibility that users could get into a use and throw mindset. This could lead to huge pile up of obsolete products in junkyards and could become a problem if they are not managed well. Hence as a best practice, OSH developers should try to promote reuse as much as possible. Not only they themselves should reuse components from junkyards, they also should develop products that can be upgraded from old products to reduce obsolescence.

4. **Modular:**

One of the best practices followed in software industry is to make the product modular so that parts of the product can be made plug and play as per customer requirement instead of forcing them to buy the entire product. This is also very relevant to OSH products as one of the key features of OSH products is to make it configurable and customize-able. Making the product modular from the idea generation stage and keeping it modular in all the subsequent steps will help in making the product easily configurable and customize-able. Making it modular helps in easy reuse as well as maintaining the product in long run.

5. **Document:**

Documentation is the last thing any developer in any field would like to do. Many of them don't understand completely the necessity for documentation and do it just for the sake of being asked to do by the quality auditors. Since in traditional product development there will be a closed knit small teams and direct involvement of these developers in post implementation phases, they may not feel the requirement for good documentation. Anyone who has tried to use a poorly documented OSH component or product would surely appreciate the requirement of good documentation. It could even determine the success or failure of an OSH product. Hence it is better to make it a practice to start documenting from the very start of the product development, so that it can be shared with OSH community regularly.

Let's now look at some of the best practices specific to OSH approach:

6. **Full collaboration:**

One of the main strength of OSH approach is collaboration. Hence you should make a practice of using this strength to the full extent. Do your homework first and then reach out – ask questions, elaborate your issues or situation, ask for suggestions and guidelines, read through as many posts as possible. People will be ready to help , share their experiences, resolve your issues, which will help in moving faster in your product development. You can also form a team of collaborators with people of similar interests, different skill-sets and experiences, so that you get parts of your product developed by other team members instead of you being a lone warrior. You can reach out for people to be your mentors or guides, so that you can use their experience and leadership. Apart from reaping the benefits of collaboration you also need to make a practice of contributing back to the OSH community. Even if you become successful and busy due to a good product, you have to make sure that you spend some time every day or regularly in answering questions, providing suggestions etc. to others who seek help. Latter on you can pick up some team or products and become mentors or guides to them.

7. **Share knowledge:**

Other important attribute of OSH is extensive sharing of knowledge. Make it a practice to share the knowledge you have gained on a regular basis. Don't wait till a phase is completed or the end of the project to share the knowledge you have gained. If you think you have gained some knowledge during any stage, that could help others, you can immediately share them. Provide as much details as you can when you share the details, as there could be different type of audiences who could be looking for different types of information. Videos, screenshots, diagrams, pictures could all help others in using the knowledge you have shared. Many of the audiences could add on to whatever you have shared, which will again help you in your product development. Documenting and sharing them when the details are still fresh in your mind is easier than waiting till the end and trying to put them together.

Above are only few areas that require best practices to be followed. Most of them are based on software industry and OSH process. You can also look at traditional processes, electronics and hardware industries to identify any best practices that can be used for OSH process as well.

CHAPTER 12

Enablers and trends in OSH

In this chapter let's look at some of the enablers and trends in the OSH world that are helping accelerated growth in OSH product development and expected to continue or increase in future. It's important to understand these enablers and trends so that readers can utilize these enablers and be prepared to take advantage of the trends. Below are some of the latest enablers and trends:

1. **Making electronics fun:**

   Hardware, especially electronics is perceived to be complex and difficult. Some of the recent component developers are trying to break this perception and make electronics and hardware fun to work with. They are making their products easy to configure and easy to program. This has led to huge fan following of these components, which is not only enabling new projects in universities but new product development by hardware enthusiasts and professionals.

2. **<u>Dynamic loading and programming capacity:</u>**

Since it's a bit difficult to play around with hardware and components, the trend is to move towards an option for dynamic loading and unloading of components and providing more features that can be programmed using software. Programming capability provided in microprocessor is already leading to accelerated adoption of OSH approach. Providing option for dynamic loading and unloading along with higher programming capability will surely lead to exponential usage of OSH approach, especially from software professionals who have some hardware related education, experience or exposure.

3. **<u>Internet of Things (IoT):</u>**

The new buzz word in high tech industry is IoT. This would require every electronics item to be connected to the internet and send relevant data either to the owners, service providers, product manufactures, data users etc. As there are millions of electronics items already in use and also being regularly being put into use, you'll need cheap components attached to these items for connecting to the internet. OSH based components are very cheap and hence many companies are starting to use this approach to make their products IoT ready. Companies like Google would like to gather as much data as possible to make their targeted ad as effective as possible and hence would be interested in investing in OSH based IoT products. Companies doing data processing of IoT data would be interested in developing cheap OSH based servers for processing their data as well.

4. **Platforms and networks:**

There are efforts by various organizations to build platforms and networks in different countries to encourage product development and manufacturing based on OSH approach as this would help to increase manufacturing activities as well as to create self-sustained communities. There are efforts to develop open source hardware parks in India, which will have hubs all across the country. There are plans to build labs, junkyards, stalls, exhibition centers, training centers, manufacturing shop floors etc. in these hubs. These hubs are expected to bring in huge number of people to get involved in OSH based product development. Other countries are expected to replicate the same model later on. Some organizations in Canada are trying to build a network of OSH professionals across the world, who would contribute towards new product development and then share the profits made by selling those products.

5. **DIY projects and OSH Kits:**

As OSH components are becoming easier to assemble and easy to program, many people are getting into Do It Yourself (DIY) type of projects.

Introduction of new types of sensors and actuators are leading to new ideas for different DIY type of projects. The information about these projects are shared online and implemented by many. Some companies have started to sell kits with different OSH components that can be configured into different products that can be used for educating or training young students or products that can be used for day-to-day use. Both these trends are leading to increase in requirement for OSH components. People tend to start using the kits first and then due to the features and potentials slowly get into DIY type of projects and later into full-fledged OSH product development.

6. **Wearable technologies:**

This is also a new trend spreading across the world. People want to wear different intelligent products on their body that can increase their appearance as well as have useful utilities. Products like smart watches, health monitoring wrist bands, powerful eye-wares, LED based display clothing are becoming very popular. Many of these products are developed using OSH based components. The product developers are planning to provide some kind of linkage to users' social networking sites directly from these wearable products which is making them even more popular among the young generation.

7. **<u>Penetration of Android</u>**

Free operating systems like Android which are developed by companies like Google are becoming very popular and the newer versions being developed can run on very small components. Many new applications are also being built on Android platform for controlling hardware components. This is leading to many new OSH products being developed and manufactured that can be easily connected to Android-based smart phones or tablets and controlled through the applications installed on these phones.

From the discussions in this chapter, it is very clear that enablers and trends indicate OSH based product development is going to be a huge area in future and everyone needs to be geared up for the same. The list is growing every day and hence we need to be aware of all the new things happening to beat obsolescence.

CHAPTER 13

Useful References

In this chapter let's look at some important areas that readers can refer to which will help them to get additional information and also to keep themselves up-to-date on relevant items related to OSH. As OSH is growing exponentially and changes happening very fast, if you don't keep yourself up-to-date, your skill-sets will become obsolete very fast, like any OSH products itself. Below are listings of some important references:

1. **OSHWA:**

   Open Source Hardware Association (OSHWA) is an international organization that has been formed to promote open source hardware and also to take up issues and interest areas pertaining to OSH space. The association is formed by volunteers who are actively working in OSH products or enthusiasts and others interested in OSH. The association is funded by membership fees and donations. The donations are eligible for tax deductions in US. They conduct many seminars and workshops across the world. They are coming up with best practices that can be followed by OSH product developers. One of the important issue in OSH space is licensing, and hence OSHWA is working in this area to help OSH enthusiasts, professionals and companies. It is suggested that all the readers become members of OSHWA and benefit from tremendous work that is being done by the board and other committees.

2. **Tindie.com**

Tindie.com is a new website launched for the sole purpose of selling OSH components. As the main objective of Tindie.com is to promote OSH based components and their manufactures, many items are sold only on Tindie.com, especially new components. It is beneficial for OSH professionals and enthusiasts to regularly browse this website to keep themselves updated on new components available, so that they can plan for new features in their products accordingly. If you have to buy any components for your product, you can do that on Tindie.com as well, as the prices are competitive.

3. **Maker**:

Maker media helps to connect makers of DIY type of products. They conduct various events for this purpose at locations across the world. Make magazine was started first to share and publish news, products and other materials about new products and mostly related to OSH. Apart from newsletters, there is a website with details about interesting items. Maker Faire is the event that is held across the world. Initially it started as a yearly event but in last couple of years multiple events are being held in different cities. An online as well as retail store named Maker Shed has been established to help makers to sell their products. This is a very good source for OSH enthusiasts and professionals to keep themselves up-to-date.

4.**Instructables**:

Instructables is a site where people upload and share details about their projects. There are options to upload documents, pictures, videos etc. Huge number of DIY project related documentation is available in this site, including many projects created using OSH components. It is suggested that the readers check first in this website for any requirements they have for any new products. Even if you don't find all the functionalities in a single project or product, you can browse for functionalities available in various projects and then include them in your product. Once you have completed your project, you can upload the details back into the website, so that others can benefit from them.

5.**OSHP of India:**

Open Source Hardware Parks (OSHP) of India is a new initiative being taken up in India to establish nation-wide hubs with OSH labs, junkyard etc.

Details of the initiative have been briefly discussed in the chapter on enablers and trends. It is suggested that the readers constantly keep updated on this initiative as many good things are expected to come out of it, and expected to be replicated in other countries as well. Many are volunteering for this initiative and have created a separate group in LinkedIn. It is suggested that the readers join this group and collaborate on this initiative.

6.**Kickstarter or Indigogo:**

These are some of the leading crowd-funding companies doing online campaigning and funding for new ideas and products. Many OSH and other product developers register their ideas and products for campaigning and funding on these websites. Browsing through the campaigns will help in knowing the trends and areas in which innovations and new ideas are being developed. There could be interesting products and components that would help your own products. You might be interested in funding them as well. In case you are developing a product and need funds to take it further, you can launch your own campaign on these websites.

7.**Books on OSH:**

There are many books that are written based on OSH related topics. These are very good reference materials for those who are interested in OSH space. Some of the organizations publish newsletters relating to innovation, DIY projects, electronics, OSH etc. These are very good sources to keep oneself updated in the ever changing, fast moving world of new technologies. Maker magazine has published many cheap books that could help in taking up easy projects. A book named 'Building Open Source Hardware' is a good book for advanced OSH product developers, which is becoming a bible for OSH world.

The above are only few references that can be used. There could be many more materials, websites, organizations etc. that could become good references for OSH enthusiasts, professionals and others interested in OSH. If readers come across any other good references, to share the same through the publishers, so that further reviews can be done and included in future versions.

CHAPTER 14

OSH Companies and products

There are many companies that are selling OSH based products and making more than $1 million in revenue. It is expected that in future, there will be many more OSH products as well as companies, and these products will have higher market share. It would be helpful for you to check out details of these companies and their products. Most of them are selling their own products which they have developed using OSH approach. There are companies that are developing and selling products that are made to work with products from other companies. Some companies are selling products of other companies through online as well as brick and mortar stores. Newer companies that provide consulting and other services to OSH companies and developers are mushrooming. Below are some examples of successful OSH companies and their products:

SparkFun: It's an electronics retailer who manufactures and sells microprocessors and breakout boards. They sell all types of components which are developed and manufactured by them as well as others to provide one stop shop for DIY enthusiasts. They also provide classes and online tutorials to educate you on electronics and other related topics.

Adafruit: It's again an online portal for learning electronics and making products, catering to makers of different ages and skills. They also include different tools, equipment and electronics that would help makers in building their own products.

Arduino: Arduino is both a company and the product developed by that company. It's an open source hardware and software company that develops cheap microprocessors that can be configured using easy-to-code software development kit. Different variations of Ardunio product are available to cater to different processing requirements. Latest one is Ardunio UNO, which has multiple digital and analog input and output pins, 16MHz resonator and USB connection to connect to your system.

BeagleBoard: It's a nonprofit organization working on educating and promoting design and use of open source hardware and software in embedded systems. It provides a forum for exchanging ideas, knowledge and experience. They have also developed, produce and sell boards that are low-cost, fan-less etc.

BugLabs: This company develops and sells open source hardware components which helps in rapid prototyping of electronic devices, mainly through lego-like hardware platform. They also develop products for enabling Internet of Things, by connecting devices to the internet.

Dangerous Prototypes: This company works on one new project every month. They post details of the project on their website and also make the assembled hardware available on Seeed Studio and other distributors for anyone to purchase. They have built many new boards and also give away free boards on a promotional basis. The blogs and forums have active following and commenting.

Olimex: One of the oldest player in open source space, they call themselves as leading provider of development tools and programs for embedded hardware. They have designed and developed many components that are used by leading electronics companies in their products. Their latest project is a single board computer named OlinuXino which can be used for building 3D printers, hosting simple scripts, home automation etc.

DIY Drones: This is a community driven organization formed for collaborative development of personal UAVs. There are details of many drones, planes, rovers etc. which are built mainly using open source hardware components. The products are available for purchase through their online store as well as distributors. Members actively participate in forum as well as blogs.

LulzBot: This is a company that builds its own 3D printers based on RepRap 3D printer specifications. You can buy the whole kit or parts. You can buy the filaments as well.

Pinoccio: This is a very new company formed for developing components for developing products with Wi-Fi capability. Due to the increase in requirement for Internet of Things enabled products, requirement for Wi-Fi components is also increasing tremendously. It also increases the portability and remote controlling capability of the products, which is also the new requirement for many products.

Evil Mad Scientist: Family owned website developing and sharing information on DIY type projects in art and education area. They have many small kits that can be used for educating kids at schools and homes as well as some kits that can be used for decorating. They provide useful feedback and comments to blogs and forums.

Liquidware: This company develops and sells display based components. These components are not only compatible with many open source hardware like Ardunio, BeagleBoard etc. but also works well with open source OS like Android. They also sell different open source components, sensors and kits.

PrinterBot: This is one more company that is developing and selling affordable 3D printers. You can buy them as kits or assembled units. The printers are more professional looking with metallic parts and enclosures.

MakerBot: One more company developing 3D printers based on RepRap design and documentation. Apart from the different hardware options, they have also developed software that can be used easily for designing and printing objects.

RepRapPro: This is a company formed by one of the inventors of RepRap 3D printers. They develop and sell all parts relating to various versions of RepRap 3D printers.

Snootlab: This company specializes in development and selling of shields for Arduino boards. All of their products are also open source based and the main objective is to provide affordable components to DIY type projects using Arduino microprocessors.

Seeed Studios: This is a company that not only sells components for DIY type projects but also has services and flexible manufacturing options to help innovators to take their product to prototyping and bigger scale production and selling.

Solarbotics: Started in 90s based on the discovery of BEAM technologies has become a major contributor in the area of robotics and also reusable solar products. Kits are available for educational purpose and also DIY projects for people with different skill-sets and different ages.

Parallax: Another company promoting all areas of electronics and DIY culture. Apart from selling components it also has online tutorials to help in improving basic skills in electronics. They also have several kits available for educational purpose as well as common DIY projects.

From the above it is clear that there are many small companies developing and selling OSH products. It's expected to continue in the same manner in the future, instead of having major companies with huge profits.

About the Author

Girish Maiya has over 17 years of experience in various fields and companies. He has worked in the areas of financial and tax audits, ERP implementation and support, software development, testing, IT Audits, SOX audits, process review and improvements. He has worked in Indian as well as multinational companies and at international locations as well. He has done consulting work for different clients in high tech as well as manufacturing industry.

Girish has been consistently providing new ideas that are practical to his senior management as well as to his clients. He has also written blogs on many of these new ideas in internal portals. Girish has been studying about different open source projects and also done some research around it. He is also working with different organizations to build a platform across various cities within India to accelerate OSH based product development and manufacturing in India. This model can be implemented across the world to benefit from collaboration and sharing.

www.ingramcontent.com/pod-product-compliance
Ingram Content Group UK Ltd.
Pitfield, Milton Keynes, MK11 3LW, UK
UKHW021342190726
13845UKWH00027B/690